THIS BOOK BELONGS TO

_____

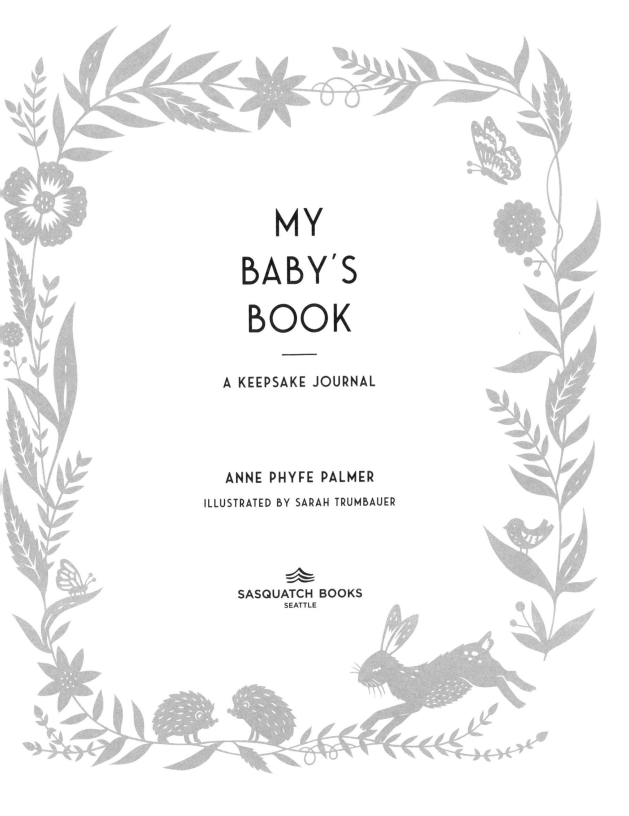

MY
BABY'S
BOOK

A KEEPSAKE JOURNAL

ANNE PHYFE PALMER

ILLUSTRATED BY SARAH TRUMBAUER

SASQUATCH BOOKS
SEATTLE

CONTENTS

HOW TO USE THIS BOOK

This book was designed for parent(s) to record the facts, details, and experiences of (and hopes for) a new baby's life. Here are some tips for how to get the most out of your time with this book:

1. Get started before baby arrives! Try to begin as soon as you have this book in your hands. Go through the whole book in advance of baby's arrival and fill in what you can; you know you will be busy soon. Keep this journal somewhere accessible to complete a prompt or two whenever you see it.

2. This book is intended to be used by families of all kinds. We have used the pronoun "we" to refer to baby's parent or parents. If baby has one parent, you can put additional photos on the second parent page or fill in the information with a godparent or close friend who has a role in baby's life.

3. If there are fewer siblings than the space allows, use the extra pages to include more photos. You might have pets instead of other children, or other people close to you, so feel free to use the sibling pages to honor those important relationships too.

4. Set calendar reminders ahead of time for the down-the-road prompts, letters from others, and annual birthday check-ins.

5. Skip questions if they are holding you up. You do not have to fill out all of the prompts! They are here to inspire, not to slow you down. If you are not ready, skip it; if it isn't pertinent, let it go.

6. Allow yourself to take several passes at each section. You might find it helpful to jump around and answer just a few prompts or questions from each section in one sitting and return another day to fill out others that speak to you. You can also ask others close to baby to help contribute as well.

7. Use the "More to Know" pages after each section to write more, add your own prompts or important information, or paste in family photos.

8. Use the Family Tree to collect information that is important to you about each family member. You could note the date of their birth or death or the location of their birth.

9. Revisit and add to this journal over months and years.

ABOUT US

PARENT

Name: ....

Nickname(s): ....

Birthdate: ....

Birthplace: ....

Astrological sign and significance: ....
....

Age on baby's due date: ....

I come from: ....
....
....

What I hope you will call me: ....

What I want you to know about my childhood: ....
....
....
....
....

What I wanted to be when I grew up and why: ....

....

Current job and how I feel about it: ....

Life dream(s): ....

....

....

How I feel about becoming a parent: ....

....

What I want you to know about me during the time you were born: ....

....

....

....

Photos of me before you arrived:

PARENT

Name: ....

Nickname(s): ....

Birthdate: ....

Birthplace: ....

Astrological sign and significance: ....
....

Age on baby's due date: ....

I come from: ....
....
....

What I hope you will call me: ....

What I want you to know about my childhood: ....
....
....
....
....

What I wanted to be when I grew up and why: ....

....

Current job and how I feel about it: ....

Life dream(s): ....

....

....

How I feel about becoming a parent: ....

....

What I want you to know about me during the time you were born: ....

....

....

....

Photos of me before you arrived:

SIBLING

Name: ....

Nickname(s): ....

Birthdate: ....

Birthplace: ....

Astrological sign and significance: ....
....

Age on baby's due date: ....

How I feel about your arrival: ....
....

Photo of me:

SIBLING

Name: ....

Nickname(s): ....

Birthdate: ....

Birthplace: ....

Astrological sign and significance: ....
....

Age on baby's due date: ....

How I feel about your arrival: ....
....

Photo of me:

SIBLING

Name: ....

Nickname(s): ....

Birthdate: ....

Birthplace: ....

Astrological sign and significance: ....
....

Age on baby's due date: ....

How I feel about your arrival: ....
....

Photo of me:

FAMILY

Before you arrived, this is what my/our life was like: ....
....
....
....
....

How we formed our family: ....
....
....
....
....

What family means to me/us: ....
....
....
....

Photos or drawings of our family before you arrived:

EXTENDED FAMILY

You are the _____ child in your family
and the _____ grandchild.

Grandparents' names and nicknames:

....

....

....

....

....

....

....

Spouse	Great-Grandparent	Grea Grandpa

Spouse	Great-Grandparent	Grea Grandpa

Spouse	Grandparent	Grandpa

Spouse	Aunt/Uncle	

Cousin(s)	Cousin(s)	Cousi

Spouse	Aunt/Uncle	

Cousin(s)	Cousin(s)	Cousi

Step-Sibling(s)	Spouse	P

Step-Sibling(s)	Sibling(s)	Si

Family Tree

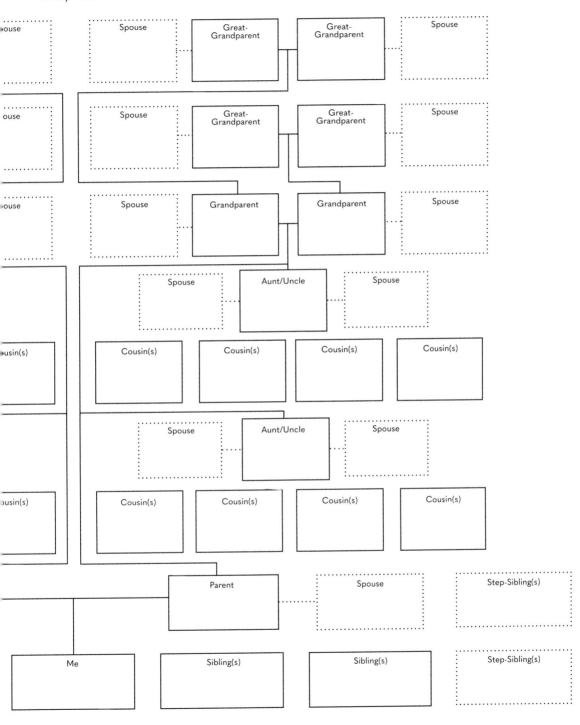

MORE TO KNOW

....
....
....
....
....
....
....
....
....
....
....
....
....
....
....

PREGNANCY

Photo of pregnancy at _____ months:

Midwife/doctor/care providers: ....

When I/we heard your heartbeat for the first time, I/we: ....
....

In utero, I/we called you: ....

To prepare for your birth, I/we: ....
....
....
....
....
....

Ultrasound or other pregnancy images:

Three words to describe this pregnancy: ....

What it felt like to be pregnant with you: ....

....

....

....

....

....

....

....

....

....

....

....

Foods I/they craved or wanted: ....

....

....

....

....

....

....

....

My/our birth plan was: ....

....

....

....

....

....

....

....

....

....

....

....

....

....

....

....

....

....

....

....

....

....

YOU'RE HERE!

How you came into the world: ....
....
....
....
....
....
....
....
....
....
....
....
....
....
....
....
....

These people helped bring you into the world: ....

....

....

These people witnessed you arrive or wanted to: ....

....

....

....

....

....

These methods/items/songs helped you come into the world: ....

....

....

In the first few hours of your life, we: ....

....

....

....

....

....

....

In the first few days of your life, we: ....

....

....

....

....

....

....

....

....

....

Some of the feelings we experienced in the first month of your life: ....

....

....

....

....

....

....

....

....

....

....

BIRTHDAY

Your birthdate and time: ....

You were born on a   M   T   W   Th   F   S   Su

You were born at: ....

Your astrological sign and significance: ....
....

The weather on the day you were born: ....

The people who helped us in your first few weeks and how: ....
....
....
....
....
....
....

The story of your umbilical cord: ....
....
....
....

Birth announcement:

Photos of our first few days:

THE DAY YOU WERE BORN

Movie(s) just released: ....

....

....

....

Popular song(s): ....

....

....

....

....

Bestselling book(s): ....

....

....

....

....

Cost of a banana: ....

Cost of a gallon of gas: ....

Cost of _____: ....

Governmental leaders: ....

Popular clothing trends: ....
....
....

Major news or headlines: ....
....
....
....
....
....

Trending on social media: ....
....
....
....
....
....
....
....

MORE TO KNOW

....
....
....
....
....
....
....
....
....
....
....
....
....
....

ABOUT YOU

NAME

Your name: ....

How we chose your name: ....
....
....

Names we considered: ....
....
....

Nicknames: ....
....

YOUR BODY

You look like: ....
....

Your eyes are like: ....
....

Your birthmarks or special features: ....
....
....

Your skin is the color of: ....
....

Your sleep patterns: ....
....
....
....
....
....

Your feeding patterns: ....
....
....
....
....
....

Your handprints in the first month of your life:

_____
date

Your footprints in the first month of your life:

_____
date

Here is what you looked like!

DRESSING YOU UP

Diapering details: ....
....

Some of your first clothing: ....
....
....

Your most comfortable outfit: ....
....

What we most liked dressing you in:

INTERACTION

You like to look at: ....
....

You are soothed by: ....
....

You are startled by: ....
....

Favorite things/people to snuggle: ....
....

What makes you smile: ....
....

What makes you giggle: ....
....

Games we play with you: ....
....

Your temperament: ....
....

Photos of you smiling, laughing, crying, or yawning:

How we know what you need: ....
....
....
....

What we call important things in your life, like blanket, pacifier, food, bottle, or milk:

....

....

....

....

NIGHT & NAPTIME

Our nighttime rituals the first year of your life: ....

....

....

....

....

....

....

....

....

How we get you to sleep: ....

....

....

....

....

Who comforts you at night and where/how: ....

....

....

....

....

You first "slept through the night" on _____, which means that:

....

....

First time in a crib: ....

....

....

First night apart: ....

....

....

....

How we put you down for naps: ....

....

....

Your nap schedules and how they changed over the first few months: ....

....

Photos of you sleepy or sleeping:

MORE TO KNOW

....

....

....

....

....

....

....

....

....

....

....

....

....

....

BABY SHOWER

Where: ....

When: ....

Who: ....

....

....

....

Games we played and stories we told: ....

....

....

....

....

Special moments: ....

....

....

....

....

....

Photos:

GIFTS

To welcome you, we received the following gifts:

Item   From

....

....

....

....

....

....

....

....

....

....

....

....

....

....

....

....

....

....

....

....

....

....

....

....

....

....

....

....

....

....

....

....

....

Most useful gift: ....

....

Most thoughtful gift: ....

....

Most humorous gift: ....

....

ATTENTION

How you are showered with attention: ....

....

....

....

....

....

....

....

How we are showered with support: ....

....

....

....

....

....

....

....

Godparents and/or special adults in your life and what they mean to us: ....

....

....

....

....

LETTERS

Our community of loved ones has these words to share with you:

Name: _____ **Relation to baby:** _____

What I see in you: ....

....

My wish for you: ....

....

My words of wisdom for you and your family: ....

....

....

Name: _____ **Relation to baby:** _____

What I see in you: ....

....

My wish for you: ....

....

My words of wisdom for you and your family: ....

....

....

Name: _____ **Relation to baby:** _____

What I see in you: ....
....

My wish for you: ....
....

My words of wisdom for you and your family: ....
....
....

Name: _____ **Relation to baby:** _____

What I see in you: ....
....

My wish for you: ....
....

My words of wisdom for you and your family: ....
....
....

Name: _____ **Relation to baby:**_____

What I see in you: ....
....

My wish for you: ....
....

My words of wisdom for you and your family: ....
....
....

Name: _____ **Relation to baby:**_____

What I see in you: ....
....

My wish for you: ....
....

My words of wisdom for you and your family: ....
....
....

Name: _____ **Relation to baby:**_____

What I see in you: ....
....

My wish for you: ....
....

My words of wisdom for you and your family: ....
....
....

Name: _____ **Relation to baby:**_____

What I see in you: ....
....

My wish for you: ....
....

My words of wisdom for you and your family: ....
....
....

Name: _____ **Relation to baby:**_____

What I see in you: ....
....

My wish for you: ....
....

My words of wisdom for you and your family: ....
....
....

Name: _____ **Relation to baby:**_____

What I see in you: ....
....

My wish for you: ....
....

My words of wisdom for you and your family: ....
....
....

CEREMONIES & RITUALS

Rituals or ceremonies we marked in the first year of your life: ....

....

....

....

....

....

....

....

Photos or programs:

MORE TO KNOW

....
....
....
....
....
....
....
....
....
....
....
....
....
....

FIRSTS

BABY

First bath: ....

....

First diaper blowout:...

....

First time with a babysitter or in daycare: ....

....

First smile: ....

....

First peek-a-boo: ....

First time you waved and to whom:...

....

First words:...

....

On our first Mother's/Father's/Parent's Day(s), we: ....

....

....

....

More baby firsts: ....

....

....

....

....

TODDLER

First tantrum:...

....

First ice cream:..

....

First friends:...

....

First playdate: ....

....

First preschool: ....
....

First song you danced to/sung:...
....

First haircut: ....
....

Lock of your hair:

More toddler firsts: ....
....
....
....
....
....
....

OUT & ABOUT

First outing: ....
....
....

First zoo visit: ....
....
....

First aquarium or beach visit: ....
....
....

First time your feet felt sand: ....
....
....

First time you touched snow: ....

....

....

First time in a lake, river, or ocean: ....

....

....

First trip to a park or playground: ....

....

....

More out-and-about firsts:..

....

....

....

....

....

....

....

....

....

....

COMMUNICATION

First signs or nonverbal cues: ....
....

First words: ....
....

First phrase or sentence: ....
....

First drawing: ....
....

More communication firsts: ....
....
....
....
....
....
....

MOVEMENT

First time you rolled over: ....
....

First time you shook a rattle: ....
....

First time you sat by yourself: ....
....

First time you crawled: ....
....

First steps and where: ....
....

First trike: ....
....

First bike with training wheels: ....

....

First bike without training wheels: ....

....

More movement firsts: ....

....

....

....

....

....

HEALTH

First doctor visit: ....

....

First illness: ....

....

....

First boo-boo: ....

....

First emergency room or emergent care visit: ....

....

Medical procedures: ....

....

First vaccinations: ....

....

....

MORE FIRSTS

First _____: ....

....

....

First _____: ....

....

....

First _____: ....
....
....

First _____: ....
....
....

First _____: ....
....
....

First _____: ....
....
....

First _____: ....
....
....

First _____: ....
....
....

MORE TO KNOW

....
....
....
....
....
....
....
....
....
....
....
....
....
....

YOUR FIRST HOME

When you were born, we brought you home to: ....

....

Description of home: ....

....

....

....

....

....

....

....

....

....

....

....

Special feature of your room: ....

....

....

Colors we surround you with: ....

....

Drawing or photo of your room:

The room in which you are most calm: ....

Animals in your home: ....
....

HOMETOWN

Your hometown, _____, is where:

....

....

....

....

Why we live(d) here: ....

....

....

Our favorite places to go in your hometown: ....

....

....

....

The state where you were born is known for: ....

....

Additional places we live(d): ....

....

....

....

....

MORE TO KNOW

....
....
....
....
....
....
....
....
....
....
....
....
....
....

SEASONS

In spring, we: ....

....

....

....

....

....

....

....

....

In summer, we: ....

....

....

....

....

....

....

....

In autumn, we: ....
....
....
....
....
....
....
....
....

In winter, we: ....
....
....
....
....
....
....
....
....

TRAVEL

First trip: ....

Trips we took in the first few years of your life: ....
....
....
....
....
....

What we want you to experience from our travels: ....
....
....

Photos from traveling:

TRANSPORTATION

Carriers we use to hold you as a baby: ....

....

To get from place to place, we use: ....

....

....

....

Our car(s) in your first few years: ....

....

....

Public transportation we use: ....

....

....

....

....

NATURE

Parks we visit: ....
....
....
....
....
....

Views we enjoy: ....
....
....
....
....

How we interact with nature: ....
....
....
....
....
....
....
....
....

MORE TO KNOW

....
....
....
....
....
....
....
....
....
....
....
....
....
....

GROWING UP

GROWTH

Growth chart

Date	Length/Height	Weight	Notes

Chart of teeth and when lost

Upper teeth

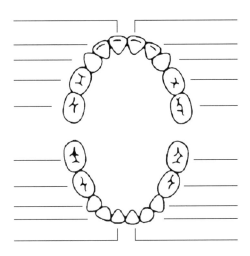

Lower teeth

NUTRITION

How we feed you as a baby: ....

....

....

How and when we introduced solid foods:..

....

Your favorite foods: ....

....

....

Photos of you eating:

YOU'RE ONE YEAR OLD!

First birthday celebration: ....

....

....

....

....

....

....

....

....

....

Measurements: ....

Foot/handprints at one year:

Current nap and sleeping schedule: ....

Your temperament: ....
....
....

What to remember about this time: ....
....
....
....
....

Favorite words: ....
....

What is most rewarding and most challenging about this time? ....
....
....
....
....
....
....

Favorite board book: ....

You in 6 words: ....
....

You in 50 words: ....
....
....
....
....

Photo, drawing, or description of you:

YOUR SECOND YEAR

Second birthday celebration: ....
....
....
....
....
....
....
....

What you are like now: ....
....

Favorite friends: ....
....

Favorite toys: ....
....

Favorite stuffed animals/dolls/objects: ....
....

Words or phrases you use: ....
....

Songs we sing: ....
....

Books we read: ....
....
....

Where we live: ....
....

Parks we visit: ....
....

Playmates:..
....

What you most enjoy:..
....

Special clothing: ....
....

A picture you drew:

Photo, drawing, or description of you:

What's happening in the world: ....
....

YOUR THIRD YEAR

Third birthday celebration: ....
....
....
....
....
....
....
....
....

What you are like: ....
....

Favorite friends: ....
....

Favorite toys: ....
....

Favorite stuffed animals/dolls/objects: ....
....

Songs we sing: ....
....

Books we read: ....
....
....

Parks we visit: ....
....

What you most enjoy:...
....

What you like to talk about: ....
....

Special clothing: ....
....

A picture you drew:

Photo, drawing, or description of you:

What's happening in the world: ....
....

YOUR FOURTH YEAR

Fourth birthday celebration: ....
....
....
....
....
....
....
....
....

What you are like: ....
....

Favorite friends: ....
....

Favorite toys: ....
....

Favorite stuffed animals/dolls/objects: ....
....

Songs we sing: ....
....

Books we read: ....
....
....

Parks we visit: ....
....

What you most enjoy: ....
....

What you like to talk about: ....
....

Special clothing: ....
....

A picture you drew:

Photo, drawing, or description of you:

What's happening in the world: ....
....

BEYOND

The values and beliefs we are sharing with you: ....

....

....

....

....

....

....

....

What we are trying to teach you as a person: ....

....

....

....

....

....

....

....

Our hopes for you: ....
....
....
....
....
....

What I/we think you might do/be when you grow up: ....
....
....
....
....

What I/we think you want to do/be when you grow up: ....
....
....
....
....

What I/we think makes you unique as a person: ....
....
....
....
....

Artwork by you:

Final thoughts as you head out of toddlerhood: ....

....

....

....

....

....

....

....

....

....

....

....

....

....

....

....

....

....

....

A letter to you from us: ....

....

....

....

....

....

....

....

....

....

....

....

....

....

....

....

....

....

....

....

....

....

....

Memorabilia:

ABOUT THE AUTHOR

ANNE PHYFE PALMER is an entrepreneur, writer, yoga teacher, sailor, electric bike commuter, and mother. She left her hometown of New Orleans for the green mountains of Vermont, where she received her BA in English and Women's Studies before heading west to Seattle and opening 8 Limbs Yoga Centers. With her guided journal series, Anne Phyfe combines her passions for self-inquiry and the written word. She lives in Seattle, and whenever possible, on the ocean. You can find her at AnnePhyfe.com. *PS: Anne Phyfe is her first name!*

ABOUT THE ARTIST

SARAH TRUMBAUER is a papercut artist and illustrator living in rural eastern Pennsylvania. Her paper cuts are inspired by long walks through gardens, vintage children's books, and art nouveau patterns. Her work has been featured in international magazines, books, and stationery products. When she's not cutting paper, she can be found drinking tea, daydreaming, and reading mystery novels with her cat, Lucy.

Printed in China

SASQUATCH BOOKS with colophon
is a registered trademark of Penguin Random House LLC

27 26 25 24 23 22   9 8 7 6 5 4 3 2 1

Editor: Jen Worick | Production editor: Peggy Gannon
Design: Alison Keefe | Illustrations: Sarah Trumbauer

ISBN: 978-1-63217-453-6

Sasquatch Books | 1325 Fourth Avenue, Suite 1025 | Seattle, WA 98101

SasquatchBooks.com

MIX
Paper | Supporting
responsible forestry
FSC® C008047